John MacMillan, Sr.

John MacMillan, Sr.

A TRUE SCOTS' LADDIE

AN IDAHO CIVIC LEADER,
A BOISE BUSINESS OWNER,
AND A WOOL GROWER.

Adell McMillan

To order additional copies of this book, contact:
Xlibris Corporation
1-888-795-4274
www.Xlibris.com
Orders@Xlibris.com
56476

CONTENTS

ILLUSTRATIONS

INTRODUCTION

I remember my grandfather, John MacMillan Sr., as a rather portly gentleman with white hair and a sizable white mustache. He moved from Boise, Idaho to live with my parents and me in 1936 when I was three years of age. Sitting at his feet I learned to talk, with him as my speech teacher!! Years later, my maternal grandmother who was an elocutionist determined that I pronounced some words not in the usual way and that I seemed to have a slight Scots' burr!! She attributed these speech anomalies to my having spent so many hours listening to my grandfather. I have long since lost the burr, but do still pronounce "out" and "about" somewhat differently!

Having researched my grandfathers' life over several years, it has seemed to me for some time that his life deserved to be preserved in a biography, which is the reason for this book project.

Adell McMillan
February 2009
Eugene, Oregon

1. "John MacMillan, Senior c.1930"

CHAPTER ONE

KIRKCUDBRIGHT

John MacMillan Sr's life began in Kirkcudbright, pronounced 'Cur-coo-bree' at Caldons in the Parish of Minigraff in the Stewertry of Kirkcudbright in South West Scotland on May 12, 1857.[1] Kirkcudbright has since become a popular and charming centre of interest. "the attraction of the little town is partly in its age. Kircudbright is a very old town and celebrated its quincentenary as a royal burgh in 1955. It is not surprising, therefore, that it is rich in history, particularly from an architectural point of view. Kirkcudbright is also famed artistically. It has long been known for the strength of local interest in art and for the popularity of its buildings and scenery depicted by many well-known artists. Artists based in Kirkcudbright can paint many landscapes and seascapes while the town itself provides popular subjects such as the harbour cottages. The inside of one of these buildings is the local art gallery where regular exhibitions are held."[2]

"The Town of Kirkudbright is finely situated on the estuary of the River Dee, and is the county town of the County or Stewartry of Kirkcudbright in South-West Scotland. Collectively with the County of Wigtown, the area was historically known as the Kingdom of Galloway, and now forms the western portion of the present-day local authority area dumfries and galloway."

"Kirkudbright is first recorded with royal Burgh status as far back as 1455, but may had had this distinction even earlier. Royal Burgh status gave the town authority to trade with ports outside of Scotland and reflected the security of its position and importance of its fine sheltered harbour."

"The original town was built around the old High Street where many old town-houses still survive. With its castle, harbour and mote, it was protecred on all sides by the tidal waters of the river dee and has prospered over many centuries since."[3]

MacMillan was born on the old homestead farm in Kirkcudbright and he "—duly availed himself of the advantages of the common schools and supplemented this discipline by a course of study in Douglass Academy, a well ordered institution. After leaving school he continued to be actively identified with agricultural pursuits in his native county for a period of four years, at the expiration of which he severed the gracious home ties to seek his fortunes in America. He is a scion of the staunchest of Scottish stock, in both the agnatic and maternal lines and is a son of Anthony and Agnes (MacFadzen) MacMillan, who joined him in Boise, Idaho in 1886, and who [there] passed the residue of their lives, the father having been a prosperous farmer in Scotland. Anthony MacMillan died in 1906 at the age of eighty-nine years, and his cherished and devoted wife did not long survive him, as she was summoned to the life eternal in 1908, at the age of seventy-seven years. Her father was an extensive farmer and influential citizen in Wigtownshire, Scotland, and attained to extremely venerable age as did also his wife. Anthony MacMillan and his wife were lifelong and zealous members of the Presbyterian church, in the faith of which they carefully reared their children, of whom five sons and three daughters[were then] "living.[4]"

CHAPTER TWO

EMIGRATION

John MacMillan emigrated to the United States of America in 1881"
on the 28th of June, four days before Garfield was shot and arrived in due
course of time in the port of New York City, whence he forthwith made
his way to the great west, concerning which he had previously informed
himself to considerable degree. Determined and ambitious, he soon found
opportunities and his initial experience was in connection with the livestock
business at Laramie, Wyoming. According to family myth, John MacMillan
Sr. Traveled across the Plains of the United States during the Sheep Wars that
grew out of disputes because of the propensity of sheep to over-graze the
range and to pollute watering places used by cattle. Some range controversies
ended in bloodshed. In Colorado, Nevada, Idaho many cowboys and
shepherds along with thousands of sheep were killed[5]. MacMillan proceeded
to Idaho in 1886, locating at Mayfield in Elmore County where he engaged
in the raising of sheep and where he remained for ten years, within which he
developed an extensive and profitable enterprise and became the owner of a
valuable estate. "In 1890 Idaho became a state and in the states first election
Mtn. Home in 1891 became the County Seat of the new Elmore County,
In 1896 Mountain Home was incorporated as a village.[6] MacMillan later
moved to Boise, where he expanded his[1] business and became a stockholder
of the company which erected and owned the magnificent Idanha Hotel[7],
one of finest in the entire northwest"[2]

THE IDANHA—THE TRAVELER'S HOME.

2. The Idanha Hotel. c.1930
"The Traveler's Home"

"In 1907 the nation's attention turned to the turreted French chateau style hotel[the Idanha] in Idaho's capital city where newsmen anxiously followed the era's most sensational trial. Labor boss Big Bill Haywood stood accused of hiring the assassin who had rigged dynamite to the gate outside [former governor] Steunenberg's Caldwell home, killing him. The 1907 trial exposed two decades of violence and intimidation over the rights of American workers and conditions in the Idaho mines."[8]

Also in 1886, John MacMillan's parents and family of Bainbridge N. Y., arrived in Boise and intended in making their home there for the future. They rented a residence of Nate Falk where the family would reside for the winter. Anthony McMillan was a viviculturist of many years experience and was desirous of buying an interest in an orchard which he was capable of managing. Their son, Thomas McMillan was one of the extensive sheep owners of Camas prairie.[5] Anthony McMillan's spouse,[Agnes McFadzen McMillan, [John McMillan's mother,] died in her seventy ninth year.

Restaurant in the Idan-ha Hotel, Boise City, Idaho, showing its Blabon floor of Linoleum—pattern 352 Inlaid.

3.The Restaurant, Idanha Hotel c.3/28/1920
"A formal dining room"

She was born in Scotland and was the second oldest in a family of 12 children all of whom but one were deceased at the time of her death. She raised a family of nine children all of whom were living at the time of her death. They were Robert McMillan of Kansas City, Mrs. Stewart of Boise, Mrs. Robert Sproat of Mayfield, Mrs Robert Aikman, John McMillan and William McMillan of Boise, Thomas McMillan and Mrs. Mayne of Mayfield and Anthony McMillan of Oregon. All were at their mother's bedside when death came except Robert McMillan of kansas City, Anthony McMillan of Oregon and Mrs. Mayne of Mayfield, who was expected to arrive in time for the funeral.[6]

John MacMillan Sr. continued his livestock interest and took an active interest in civic affairs. He erected a fairgrounds where animal livestock shows were held.

On the occasion of the State Fair and a visit of a delegation from Salt Lake City to Boise, the *Idaho Statesman* carried an article titled "Salt Lakers

Speak Well of Boise": "Hospitality is a trademark in the town of Boise, and its leading citizens have the spirit of progress, younger lights having crowded out the old mossbacks who formerly did so much to keep it off the map. Men like President John McMillan . . . seem to hold the public reins and are urging the town forward in a manner that shows results." "Boise has a natural attraction, a fine natatorium and as a curiosity a good hotel. It will surely succeed."

MacMillan immediately became active in politics after arriving in Boise and was a member of the Senate from Ada County in 1909. He had previously served as a representative from Elmore County. He received his commission as Postmaster in Boise on February 18, 1910. He was a charter member of the Boise Lodge of the Elks and served at one time as exalted ruler of the Elks. Additionally, MacMillan was a member of the Methodist Episcopal Church.[7]

CHAPTER THREE

NATURALIZATION

According to his naturalization papers, John MacMillan "In district court of the Second Judicial District, in and for the county of Ada, Territory of Idaho, presented himself before the Honorable Judge James H. Beatty in the matter of his application in open court in the March term 1890 to become a Citizen of the United States on the 15th day of March 1890 "It appearing to the satisfaction of this court, by the oaths of David Falk and Hosia B. Eastman, citizens of the United States of America, witnesses for that purpose, first duly sworn and examined, that John MacMillan, a native of Great Britain, has resided within the limits and under the jurisdiction of the United states five years at least, last past, and within the Territory of Idaho for one year at least, last passed; and that during all of said time he has behaved as a man of good moral character, attached to the principles of the Constitution of the United States and well disposed to the good order and happiness of the same; and it also appearing to the Court by competent evidence, that said applicant has heretofore, and more than two years since, and in due form of law, declared his intention to become a citizen of the United States; and having now here, before this Court, taken an oath that he will support the Constitution of the United States of America, and that he doth absolutely and entirely renounce and abjure all allegiance and fidelity to every foreign Prince, Potentate, State or Sovereignty whatever and particularly to The Queen of Great Britain of whom he was a subject. It is therefore ordered, adjudged and decreed, that the said, John Macmillan be and is hereby admitted and declared to be a Citizen of the United States of America. [signed] by Judge James H. Beatty[8]

CHAPTER FOUR

MARRIAGE AND FAMILY

John MacMillan married Miss Clara Hubbell, daughter of Norman S. Hubbell, a representative citizen of Boise, on Movember 20, 1896. Clara for years was one of the leading hostesses of Boise. Her spacious home on Franklin Street was the center of much hospitality. She was a member of the First Methodist church. Clara MacMillan was born at Union, Oregon and was reared and educated in Boise, Idaho. Family myth has it that Clara was the first white child born west of the Continental Divide!

Clara, age 61, "died unexpectedly at her home in Boise from a stroke of apoplexy. She had suffered a similar stroke six years prior[to her date of death,] but recovered and her health in recent years had been considered excellent. She telephoned her husband at a hotel in Boise that she was suffering from a severe headache. She died a short time after he reached home with a doctor. Besides her husband, John MacMillan Sr., she was survived by two brothers Walter Hubbell, Los Angeles and Norman S. Hubbell, Boise."[9]

John and Clara MacMillan had one son, John Jr. Who was born on the 28th of March 1897. He was a member of the class of 1915 of Boise High School.[10] John Jr. served in the military in World War 1 and returned to Boise in 1918. "has arrived home from Charleston, S.C. McMillan has been serving on the U. S. S. West Loquassuck. He just returned from a cruise to Chile. His ship passed through the Panama Canal. He has received his discharge from the Navy. McMillan is a well known and popular Boise boy."[11]

John Jr. married Eunice Adale Hoyt on April 15, 1932, and they had one child, a daughter, whom they named Adell, born June 22, 1933.

John Srs' brother William,62, died in June of 1935 at a Boise hospital of anemia, from which he had suffered for some six months. He had been a Boise resident since 1886 and was survived by Thomas McMillan, John McMillan and Mrs. Robert Aikman of Boise, Mrs. Jane Stewart[12] of Portland; Mrs. Jessie King Mayne of Chula Vista, California, and Antony McMillan, Reno, Nevada.[13]

"Robert Aikman, one of the pioneer business men of Boise, died at a Boise hospital . . . after an illness of nearly two years. Mr.

Aikman was born in Scotland June 26, 1852, and came to Idaho in 1882 having located first in Canada. His arrival was simultaneous with another group of Scotch whom he had not known in the old country, but with whom he soon became acquainted and married the sister of John and Thomas McMillan."

"Although engaged in the live-stock business from the start, Mr. Aikman was also interested in many other community projects. He was one the original stock holders and active managers of the Idanha Hotel and had been for years interested in the Boise Stone Company. He served as councilman under Harry Fritchman and through his residences in Boise was keenly interested in civic affairs."

"He was a member of Boise Lodge No. 310 Elks and the Independent Order of Odd Fellows at Caldwell. He is survived by his widow, one son, Robert Aikman, Jr. And one daughter, Mrs. James Spofford of Mountain Home, also five grandchildren, one sister, Miss Nellie Aikman and two brothers, George and Henry Aikman, all of Scotland . . ."[14]

CHAPTER FIVE

IDAHO WOOL GROWERS

John MacMillan Sr. over a period of several years was very active in the Idaho Wool Growers Association, serving as its' president at one time. During his work with the wool growers he became embroiled in a controversy over the existence of Scab within the sheep growing business in Idaho. This activity was the basis for an extensive column in the *Idaho Statesman* (date unknown) as follows:

"Scab and Scabby":

"Mr. John McMillan, president of the Idaho Wool Growers association, is happy in the possession of an excellent heart, but unfortunate inasmuch as the operations of his mind are not always directed by that organ. This is not only a misfortune, but really an extraordinary circumstance, for, while a good brain is often associated with a malevolent heart, it is seldom, indeed, that the order is reversed. We feel sure, though, that only a very small portion of Mr. McMillans' brain is affected. One cell, it would seem is still subject to the hypnotic power of his distinguished Secretary.

A week or ten days ago this malign influence seems to have had all of Mr. McMillans' faculties in subjection and it prompted him to say things, which, for his own peace of mind we hope he may be quite unable to recall upon regaining normal consciousness.

During this period of passivity, acting through suggestion, Mr. McMillan gave a Boise newspaper an interview reflecting seriously upon the official character of Mr. J. C. Dressler, State Sheep Inspector. He was made to charge, indirectly, that Mr. Dressler is not a fit person to hold the office of inspector and in consequence of this unfitness, the sheep of Idaho are become sorely afflicted of the scab. He also, indirectly charged that governor Morrison is guilty of culpable indifference to the distress of the sheep and misfortune of their owners. He said that heretofore when the sheep became scabby all he had to do was mention it to the governor and the thing was attended to forthwith. That was certainly very nice of former governors, and no doubt any good governor, on being appraised of the existence of sab, would drop everything else, get him a tub of dip and go forth to exterminate the disorder. But, it appears, that in the present emergency, Mr. McMillan failed to give governor Morrison an opportunity to emulate the benevolent spirit of his predecessors; for, instead of informing his excellency of the state of affairs, he sought out a newspaper reporter and poured into his sympathetic ear the scabby tale of woe. This was not like John McMillan. He would never rob a governor of an opportunity to distinguish himself and then complain because the distinguishing act was not performed. But let that go.

Mr. McMillan seeks to spread the impression that the scab among Idaho sheep results from the inefficient administration of the Inspecters' office. If our memory serves us right, Mr. Dressler was appointed in pursuance of a formal resolution of the Idaho Wool Growers' association. The president of the association is therefore acting in bad taste when he condemns the appointment without the same authority that recommended it; and he is certainly laying himself justly liable to a charge of meanness when he seeks to discredit Governor Morrison because of it. Mr. McMillan is, normally, too big and generous a man to do things like that.

Scab is a calamitous thing, but primarily, those who suffer from it are responsible for it. We never knew a citizen, however depraved, to poison the ranges with scab unless he was a sheepman. Why doesn't President McMillan hunt out the members of his Association who committed this act of perfidy and visit just punishment on them? True, this might involve the president himself, but a little thing like that would not deter John McMillan from laying the ax to the root of the evil.

As to Mr. Dressler, we don't personally know a single thing about his official conduct, but we know the man, and, therefore, we know that when the record is made up it will put to shame his maligners. You will hunt the country over and fail to find a squarer or more conscientious man, and some day when McMillans' heart resumes control of his mental faculties, it will grieve him to think that he ever figured as an accuser of J. C. Dressler".[15]

CHAPTER SIX

MEETING OF WOOL GROWERS
(December 9, 1902)

Idaho Association Convenes and Elects delegates to Kansas City

---

Old Officers Unanimously Elected

"Convention marked by harmonious action on all matters—address by President McMillan, Report of secretary MontieB. Gwinn, and address of Professor Henry Slade of the State University all of special interest.

"On motion the special meeting was made regular in order that the annual election of officers might take place and that other business might be attended to. On motion of F. R. Gooding a committee on order of business was appointed by the chair, consisting of F. R. Gooding, J. D. Wood and R. F. Cooke. There being nothing before the meeting, President McMillan said he would take up the time by delivery of his address. He spoke as follows:"

PRESIDENTS' ADDRESS by John MacMillan Sr.

"Gentlemen, Members of the Idaho Wool Growers' Association: A little over 12 months ago it was my privilege to call your attention to the sound financial standing and excellent showing of our association. I am now pleased to report to you a continuation of these satisfactory conditions. In fact, considering the circumstances, I think we have made a marvelous growth during the past year. All our old members are still with us, and to think that since our last meeting we have added 170 to our membership and the active interest and unanimity of opinion which prevails among our members show conclusively that they appreciate the advantages to be derived from our strong organization and determination to maintain the Idaho Wool growers' association where and that it is the strongest association of its kind in the United States."

"Since our last meeting the delegates appointed by you at the time attended the meeting of the National Live Stock Association[16] in Chicago. There many questions of importance to the live stock interests can be presented by an individual member or by the representative of some association who is a member of the executive committee and if deemed worthy of consideration will by them be recommended to the association for its action."

"The "anti-shoddy bill" which originated in this association was favorably acted upon by the National Live Stock Association, afterward introduced in congress by Representative Grosevenor of Ohio and although failed to pass at the last session of congress, I believe it will during the present term, although its passage is stubbornly resisted by the friends of the manufacturers."

"During the meeting of the National Live Stock Association at Chicago, the delegates in attendance had the privilege of attending the meeting of the International Live Stock Exposition, the greatest show of the kind in the world, a description of which I have not time to give, only that it is well worth a visit from any one interested in the business, and where a member of our association had the honor of winning first prize on a carload lot of Idaho raised lambs."

"Idaho is one of the strongest supporters that the National Live Stock Association has, and when it comes to a vote the state of Idaho is always in the lead, having more votes than any other state represented; and owing to the strength and influence the National Live Stock Association has with reference to any matter brought before congress. I believe it to be for our advantage to advance and maintain our friendly relations with that association."

"During the convention the delegates from our association attended a meeting of the National Wool Growers' Association at which a subscription of $300 was made for the purpose of furthering our interests and assisting in the hard and effective work being done by the president of the association, Senator Warren of Wyoming."

"In matters of litigation our attourney has been kept busy attending to business for the association. The case of Sweet vs. Ballentyne was argued in the Supreme Court and decided against us; application was made for a rehearing and denied. This case is now appealed to the United States Supreme Court for their decision. Many other cases on the two-mile limit law have been presented, and in nearly all advice has been given as to the the proper conduction of such cases. In the case of Smith vs. Lowe we have so far been successful. The case, however, having been appealed and argued before the United states Court of Appeals in San Francisco a few days ago and from which court there has been no decision. In the matter of Lewis, who obtained judgement against this association in Colorado court for over $700, a compromise was effected and final settlement made upon payment by us of $100."

"However, notwithstanding some local disturbances, I believe that the present condition of the sheep business is very satisfactory. The greatest loss and inconvenience we had to contend with during the past year was occasioned by the scarcity of cars to carry our fat stock to market, it being nothing uncommon for a flock master to order his cars six weeks before shipping, cut out and drive his stock to the shipping point and then find that he could not get cars for two or three weeks, causing the necessity of holding prime stock upon a range when short feed and a scarcity of water prevailed until his stock when shipped went on the market as ordinary feeders instead of topping market as they ought to, and would have had they been shipped at the proper time. In order to overcome this loss, I believe that every sheep owner ought to send at once to the secretary of this association the number of sheep he intends to ship and month in which he intends to ship then a tabulated form could be sent to the railroad officials showing the number of cars necessary to properly carry the shipment and by that means enable them to make preparations for the successful handling of this immense business as unfortunately for the sheep man this scarcity of cars caused the loss of thousands of dollars to them."

"One of the principle causes of loss to stock men in the west arises from what has heretofore received the scant consideration viz: poisonous plants and their history. The loss in Idaho to sheep men only by poison during this past 12 months would amount to at least $20,000. This loss has been equally as large in Montana, but government has become interested and is carrying on a series of experiments collecting the specimens of the poisonous plants and roots, and by analysis determining the poison and finding an antidote. Loses have been so heavy in Idaho this year that I had the contents of the stomachs of some of the sheep that died sent to the University of Idaho in Moscow. The contents were turned over to Professor Slade of the experimental station for analysis, who reported that he found traces of poison, but no traces of any saltpeter. The case has, moreover, aroused such an interest that I am pleased to say Professor Slade is with us today and has with him some specimens of poisonous plants which will prove of interest. Professor Slade is here to discuss this matter and assist this association any way possible and I believe that by proper investigation at different times of the year great good can be accomplished."

"Owing to the action of this association in paying the expenses of Mr. Braley and Mr. Lowe to quietly make an examination in the Utah sheep early last spring, I am glad to report that the conditions of sheep within the state of Idaho so far as freedom from desease is concerned make an excellent showing. The thanks of the association are due to Governor Hunt for rendering his assistance wherever needed, and particularly so by his readiness to issue proclamations against the importation of diseased ship or sheep from an infected territory wherever he was shown conclusively that such action was necessary to protect the flocks of Idaho from contagion. A fortunate selection has been made in the office of state sheep inspector, as the present satisfactory condition of our sheep is due to the energetic and never-tiring energy and hard work done by our present inspector, Mr. T. G. Lowe, and as the success of the sheep business in the future depends to a great extent upon the strict enforcement of the law relating to scab, I hope that Governor—elect Morrisen, when he assumes the reins of government will be equally fortunate in the selection of an Inspector who will perform the duties of his office without fear or favor."

"Another subject of great importance to sheepmen seems to be looming up in the near future. In these days of consolidation and centralization of great enterprises that of the entire control of the fat live stock price is about to be arranged. Whereby the price of all meat products will be determined by one man, who shall have absolute control, and from whose verdict we can have no redress. For that reason I believe that the sale of all our sheep should be made through one particular concern, who should have no equal show in establishing prices as the price would then be agreed upon between two men who would be on equal grounds. An immense concern organized upon proper lines could to a great extent control the supply, not with any expectation of advancing prices, but with the intention of maintaining steady prices as with present conditions a gutted market one day and a short supply the next is the prevailing occurrence and all the loss from such unsteadiness falls upon the shipper, as the consumer pays steady prices. The sole object of this suggestion is to devise some ways and means to prevent the occurrence of such an unmerciful slump in prices as occurred during the month of June of this year whereby the price of mutton declined $2 per hundred in two or three days and the unfortunate shipper of whose sheep were offered after the decline received for his sheep in the market $1 per head less than his sheep were worth on the range. This suggestion is made for your consideration and possibly with your assistance we may devise a solution of this problem."

"The unprecedented success and credit for the continued interest in this association led to a great extent with our active and energetic secretary. No one man has done more to bring this association to its present prosperous condition than Mr. Gwinn. In his travels over the state he is continually at work talking over the advantages of the association and getting new members at every trip. The amount of work that is done through the secretarys' office is astonishing: circular letters are sent out by the thousands and the amount of money handled is almost $50,000 per year. Upon the ledger there are about 450 accounts.

Every communication has been answered by return mail, and on matters of importance a meeting of executive committee is always called, causing more work as at every meeting of the executive committee proper minutes are kept. This association has, however, outgrown its scanty office provisions and in order to keep up with our progress it will be necessary to allow Mr. Gwinn sufficient money to employ a competent bookkeeper, as the work heretofore has always been done gratis by our secretary, the money allowed being only enough to pay for the work done by a stenographer. The financial condition of our association is very satisfactory and I will therefore let our secretary embody in his report the details."

"In conclusion, I may say that I deem it necessary to call the attention of our members to the many advantages and profits they realize through this association, and to request of every member to stand by and work for the association in the future the same as they have done in the past, and that means help to promote the welfare and usefulness of the association."

(The address was listened to with great interest and after its close the secretary and treasurer made reports.)"

ELECTION OF OFFICERS.

The election officers for the association was then taken up. The principal officials were elected unanimously as follow:

President—John McMillan vice President—L. L. Ormsby
Secretary and treasurer—Montie B. Gwinn
Esecutive Committee—Fred W. Gooding, J.E Glinton, Jr., F. J. Hagenbarth and Robert Aikman

Vice Presidents for the different counties were elected as follows:
Ada—Josept Pence
Boise—samuel ballantyne
Bingham—James E. Steele
Bannock—D. Douglass
Bear Lake—John Grimmith[17]

MacMillans' Political Life and Friends

GOVERNOR SHOUP'S SUPPORTERS FOR U. S. SENATOR IN THIRD SESSION
OF STATE LEGISLATURE

Reading from left to right—Top, Senator Vic Bierbower, Logan county., leader of the Shoup caucus in the senate.   Second row—Representative T. Wyman, Ada county, leader of the Shoup caucus in the house; Representative S. E. Vance, Lemhi county.   Third row—Representative John McMillan, Elmore county; Representative Thomas A. Davis, Monida county, only Democrat in the house; Representative Thomas Elder, Lemhi county.   Fourth row—Representative Charles A. Brown, Elmore county; Senator J. W. Cunningham, Ada county.   Fifth row—Senator George D. Golden, Elmore county; Representative Joseph B. Daly, Ada county; Representative Irv. Johnson, Blaine county. Sixth row—Representative Francis Flitner, Washington county; Representative John L. Baxter, Logan county.   Bottom—Representative Glenn, Boise county.

6. Supporters of Gov. Shoup.
"Supporters of Gov.Shoup for U. S. Senator in Third Session of
Idaho State Legislature, including John MacMillan Senior."

The story of John MacMillan Srs' life would not be complete without mention of his political career and especially his close friends in politics, in particular U.S. Senator William E. Borah.

A column in the *Idaho Daily Statesman* carried an invitation to one and all to attend a grand reception for Idaho's next U. S. Senator: "Popular Informal Gathering at Idanha Tonight Where Citizens May Meet and congratulate Hon. W. E. Borah—all welcome."

"The reception was under the direction of the legislative entertainment committee of the Commercial Club of the city[Boise] and it was noted that the reception was "strictly informal", and as one member of the committee expressed it, "there will be no kid gloves." and as the "presence of ladies is especially desired and is urged by the committee in charge." John MacMillan was listed with others as members of the reception committee.[18]

John McMillan began his legislative career in the Third Session of the Idaho legislature. A column in the *Idaho Statesman* (date unknown) described that beginning as follows:

"The Scotch part of the Ada county delegation in the house is John McMillan of Boise, chairman of the committee on banks and banking and a member of the livestock and fish and game committees.

"He fought enthusiastically for the state fair bill defeated by the house. He believes in fairs. He was president for several years of the I daho Intermountain Fair Association.

"Mr. McMillan was born in Scotland in 1857 and came to America when 24 years of age. He settled in Elmore county in 1886, coming to Idaho from Laramie, Wyo. And was engaged in sheep raising there until 1894. His legislative experience began in that period, also for he was a representative from Elmore county in the third session. In the ninth session he was senator from Ada county.

"During the Taft administration Mr. McMillan was postmaster of Boise. He has been president of the Idanha Hotel company ever since that popular hostelry was built. For several years he was president of the idaho wool growers association. He is a member of the Kiwanis club of Boise and a past exalted ruler of Boise Lodge No. 310 B.P.O.elks."[19]

Senator William E. Borah

Because William E. Borah was a close friend and associate of John MacMillan, Senior, it was important to include information about the life and times of Borah.

"William E. Borah was born in Fairfield, Wayne county, Illinois, June 29, 1865 was of German and Irish linage.

William N. Borah, his father, was a native of Kentucky. His mother was Elizabeth West, a native of Indiana.

He was raised on the old family homestead in Illinois, where he entered the Southern Academy at Enfield, where he studied a year, afterward matriculating at the university at Lawrence, Kan.

He later went to Lyons, Kan. where he began reading law under the instruction of A. M. Lasley, now of Chicago. In 1888 he was admitted to the bar.

"He came to Boise in 1891 and began the active practice of his profession in which he rose rapidly until he is now one of the most successful lawyers in the northwest.

On April 28,1895, Mr. Borah married Miss Mamie McConnell, daughter of ex-Governor W. J. McConnell of Idaho".[20]

WILLIAM E. BORAH.
Yesterday Elected by the Idaho Legislature as United
States Senator to Succeed Hon. Fred. T. Dubois.

1906-7

5.William E. Borah c.1906-7
"Elected by the Idaho Legislature as United States Senator
to succeed Hon.Fred T. Dubois."

"In 1894, Borah became chairman of the Republican State Central Committee. He won election to the U.S. Senate in 1906 and was returned to office five times by large majorities, making his tenure one of the longest in U.S. history. Borah's distrust of government centralization limited his commitment to social reform, but he did sponsor bills establishing the Department of Labor as well as the federal Children's Bureau. He also strongly supported the federal income tax and fought the trusts."[21]

"Isolationism dominated Borah's attitudes toward foreign policy. He did, however sponsor a congressional resolution (19221) calling for an international naval disarmament conference in Washington D.C., resulting in the naval Armament Limitation Treaty concluded Feb. 6, 1922. Assuming the chairmanship of the Senate Committee on foreign Relations in 1924, he wielded enormous power in this area for the next 16 years.

"Borah did not object to international compacts so long as the enforcement mechanism was limited to moral sanctions; thus he lent his support to the Kellogg-Brand Act (Paris, 1928)—an effective multilateral agreement theoretically outlawing war as an instrument of national policy. He consistently upheld diplomatic recognition of the Soviet Union and also helped establish the Good Neighbor policy toward Latin America by advocating a fair deal for Mexico during the controversy over foreign held oil properties (1926-28).

"During the Great depression of the 1930s, Borah supported many New Deal measures designed to relieve internal economic conditions. As European tensions mounted, however, he held fast to his isolationist stance by resisting all attempts to involve the U. S. On the side of the Allies."[22]

Borah's election to the U.S. Senate came about as a result of the Idaho legislature electing him to succeed Hon.Fred T. Dubois. Borah's nomination to the Senate was seconded by John McMillan, whose seconding the nomination speech read as follows:

"Mr. President and fellow senators, on behalf of Ada County I desire to second the nomination of W. E. Borah to the senate of the United States."

"In Mr. Borah we have a man well qualified to perform the arduous duties of a statesman, a man of deep research and excellent judgment, studious by nature and with a faculty of remembering what he reads, his mind a perfect storehouse of knowledge, he possess all the qualifications of being a leader among men. And the state of Idaho, through having such a representative will be brought more prominently before the world, than at any previous time in its history."

"Events of an unusual nature have taken place within our borders during the past two years, so that, the eyes of the whole civilized world have been riveted upon us, some of which have been satisfactorily settled, while others are progressing towards a successful termination, but there is nothing which could be done which would have more especially restore the confidence of the people than in electing such an able representative to the United States Senate.

"A man who, from his position from the floor of the Senate would, by his eloquence, be able to refute the false acccusations and misrepresentations that have been made against the fair citizens of Idaho by those high in authority, during the past several months."

"A most successful lawyer, standing easily at the head of his profession with a practice that brings him a princely income, he is willing to sacrifice all in order that he may serve the people of his state. In honoring W. E. Borah the citizens of Idaho do honor to themselves.

"A man who has taken a leading part in every campaign since becoming a resident of the state. A man who, by his pleasant smile and magnetic personal charm, has gained the confidence and respect of the citizens of Idaho, we send him forth for greater worlds to conquer, confident in his ability to mount step by step until he reaches the highest pinnacle in the ladder of fame.

"Fellow senators, I have much pleasure in seconding the nomination for the office of United States senator of the last Republican state convention, the unanimous choice of the joint Republican caucus of the ninth legislative assembly, the most popular citizen of the state of Idaho, my fellow townsman, friend and neighbor, W. E. Borah."[23]

In addition to Borah, the name of Hon. Fred T. Dubois was also placed in nomination for the office of Unites States Senator. After a roll call vote, Borah was elected by a vote of 15 for Borah and 6 for Dubois.[24]

4.Hon. John McMillan c. 1906
"Secretary of the Inaugural Ball Committee"

Serving as Idaho's U.S. Senator for 33 years, Borah is best known for his major role at the end of World War 1 (1918) in preventing the United states from joining the League of Nations and the World Court.[25]

Pigeon Shoot

On the occasion of a visit to Twin falls, Idaho by the members of the Idaho Legislature, many visited Twin Falls and others took part in a Pigeon Shoot at the Gun Club Grounds. "Senator McMillan proved himself an adept, getting six out of one ten, five in another and then six more. In the sneak shoot he showed the spectators that he has been in brush with a gun for he killed three out of five flushed."[26]

Baked Potato Worshippers

"John McMillan, one of the members [from] Boise, also postmaster, protector and defender of the faith, regrets his inability to be present at the breakfast. He says, "There's a reason." And gives it thus:

To the Distinguished Independent Order Baked Potato Worshippers, Twin Falls chapter Number One:

"I'm very sorry that I cannot attend breakfast. "There's a reason. Potatoes are fattening, and I'm too fat. Twin Falls potatoes would make me "bust my suspenders." Yours with Thanks, John McMillan."[27]

CHAPTER SEVEN

FINLAYSTONE HOUSE

Clan MacMillan's current home in Scotland, Finlaystone House, is located on the southern bank of the Firth of Clyde, west of Glasgow and not far east of Port Glasgow.[28] The famous John Knox Tree stands at the right corner of the house.[29]

"A more elegant mansion was created in the mid-18th century and today, after a series of alterations and a late Victorian make over, it is a splendid Scottish Baronial mansion in superb position overlooking the Clyde, surrounded by truly beautiful gardens and grounds.[30]

CHAPTER EIGHT

CLAN MACMILLAN

Throughout this biography the author has used the spelling of the family name as it was spelled by her father and grandfather. However, in researching the background history of the family, it appears that the correct spelling would have been "MacMillan." In fact John MacMillan Seniors' Naturalization [Citzenship] papers use the traditional "MacMillan"[31] spelling rather than "McMillan."[32]

Meaning "Children of the Tonsured Servant," "an indication that their progenitor may have been a churchman of note way back in the day when Scotlands' mainland was the mission field of the Celtic church. His identity is lost in the mists of time but the name 'Malcoluim Mac Molini' is recorded as a witness to the grant of lands 'to Christ, and to Dostan, and to Columcille'in a Gaelic marginal note in the Book of Deer, that manuscript written between the ninth and twelfth century in the Celtic religious settlement in Aberdeenshire, which came to light in the library of the University of Cambridge in 1860"[33].

"Tradition has it that the MacMillans were among the natives of the old Kingdom of Moray whose rebellious spirit was subdued in the reigns of Malcolm IV and David I by scattering them and replacing their leaders with Norman barons. Moray at that period covered a wide area and it may be that only the peoples in the eastern parts were uprooted. At any rate MacMillans remained in pockets along the north-west side of the Great Glen from Glen Urquhart to the west coast, the greatest concentration being around Loch Arkaig. The fighting skill of the MacMillans was made good use of by Somerled of the Isles who for long aided the claim of the descendants of the Maermors of Moray to the Scottish Throne. The Lords of the Isles in their turn were well served, and, with the passage of time, as the Clann Ghille Mhoil Aberach, the MacMillans of Lochaber became henchmen of the Camerons of Lchiel."[34]

THE BICYCLE CONNECTION

"The world's first pedal bicycle was made by a Dumfriesshire blacksmith Kirkpatrick MacMillan in 1836. His novel design enabled cyclists to ride with both their feet continuously off the ground for the first time; the popular bicycle of the time, the Hobby Horse, only provided momentum through the swinging of the riders feet back and forth. MacMillan never patented his idea and it was therefore widely copied. In June 1842 MacMillan, who was known locally as 'Daft Pate,' decided to visit his brother in Glasgow on his bicycle, a distance of 68 miles. However when he reached the Gorbels he knocked down a little girl who ran across his path and he was fined five Scots shillings for speeding at eight mph. The magistrate initially declared that the highways of Britain had to be kept free of 'speedsters' of his kind but later modified his opinion and is said to have slipped him the money for the fine."[35]

CHAPTER NINE

POET AND SONG WRITER

Among his other talents, John MacMillan,Senior was a published poet and song writer. Several of his poems were published in the *Idaho Statesman* newspaper. Though many were published as anonymous, many friends appeared to know who the author was.

One poem/song was as follows:

SCOTLAND DEAR SCOTLAND I LOVE THEE
By John McMillan[36]

Oh Scotland, my own, how I love thee,
Although wafted by fortune away;
From mem'ry naught e'er can efface thee,
E'en though pleasures and pastimes be gay.
In the days of my youth I wandered
O'er thy heathery mountains and hills,
Where beauties of nature abounded
In thy waterfalls, lakes, glens and rills

Chorus

Oh Scotland, dear Scotland, I love thee,
Tho I've wandered so far from my home;
for memory ne'er ne'er shall forget thee,
Oh Scotland, dearest Scotland, my own.

In Life's sunny days I did leave thee,
Mid many a fond loving adieu;
and oh! But my heart it beat sadly,
As thy shores slowly faded from view.
And yet when my heart was the saddest,
My innermost prayer was just then
To God, in his merciful kindness,
Let me visit thy dear shores again.

Chorus

But now as I look to'rd the future,
And wonder what the fates have in store;
New hopes and ambitious possess me,
Ere I land on America's shore.
And yet, with new customs prevailing,
New work and new duties in view,
Midst pleasures and joys most alluring,
Dear Scotland I still think of you.

Chorus

And so after long years of reading,
While thy hist'ry to me seems so grand;
Your statesmen and soldiers are making
Noble records by which you can stand.
New ties have been fashioned since then,
As God had dealt kindly unto me,
I will visit they dear shores again.

Chorus

A second version of the above, titled just "SCOTLAND" reads as follows:

SCOTLAND

Second Version

Oh Scotland, dear, I love thee,
tho wafted by time away,
From memr'y naught can efface thee,
Tho pleasures be so gay.
I' the days of youth I wandered,
O'er thy heathery mounts and hills,
Where nature rich abounded,
Thy lakes and glens and rills.

Chorus

Oh, Scotland dear, I love thee
Tho I've wandered far from home;
I never shall forget thee,
Oh Scotland, dear, my own.

In sunny days I left thee,
Mid many a fond adieu
And oh, my heart beat sadly,
Thy shores had faded from view;
Yet when my heart was saddest,
My inmost prayer was then
To God, in his loving kindness,
To see thy shores again.

Chorus

So after years of reading,
Thy history seems so grand,
Thy brave and noblest are making,
A record which will stand;
Tho long ago I left thee,
New ties have wrought since then,
As God hath dealt so kind to me,
I'll see thy shores again.

Chorus

Other Poems by John MacMillan, Sr. :

The Land of the Heather

Life's sunny days I did Leave thee,
Mid many a fond adieu;
And Oh! But my heart it beat sadly,
As thy shores slowly faded from view.
And yet when my heart was the saddest,
My innermost prayer was just then
To God, in his merciful kindness,
Let me visit thy dear shores again.

The years that have gone have been busy,
Of knocks I have had my share;
While honors conferred have been many,
With my friends I will gladly compare.
This country for health and for pleasure,
For hurry and bustle and gain,
My friends I consider a treasure,
But for Scotland my love I'll retain.

And now after long years of reading,
Thy hist'ry to me seems grand,
For statesman and soldiers are making
Noble records by which you can stand.
So now, though it's long since I left thee,
As god unto me hath dealt kindly,
Let me visit thy dear shores again.

Chorus:

Oh, scotland; dear Scotland, the land o' the heather,
The land o' the brave and true,
Where with primrose and daisies and bluebells to gather,
Old Scotland, I still think of you.

ADDRESS TO HAGGIS

Fair fa' your honest, sonsie face,
Great chieftain o' the pudding-race!
Aboon them a'ye tak your place,
                   Painch, tripe, or thairm:
Weel are ye wordy o' a grace
                   As lang's my arm.

The groaning trencher there ye fill,
Your hurdies like a distant hill
Your pin wad help to mend a mill
                   In time o' need,
While thro' your pores the dews distil
                   Like amber bead.

His knife see rustic labor dight,
An' cut you up wi' ready sleight,
Trenching your gushing entrails bright,
                   Like any ditch;
And then, O what a glorious sight,
                   Warm-reekin, rich!

Then, horn for horn, they stretch an' strive:
Deil tak the hindmost~ on they drive,
Till a' their weel-swall'd kytes belyve
                   Are bent like drums;
Then auld Guidman, maist like to rive,
                   'Bethanket!' hums.

Is there that owre his French ragout,
Or olio that wad staw a sow,
Or fricassee and mak her spew
                   Wi' perfect scunner,
Looks down wi' sneering, scornfu' view
                   On sic a dinner?

Poor devil! See him owre his trash,
As feckless as a withered rash,
His spindle shank, a guid whip-lash,
                His nieve a nit;
Thro' bluidy flood or field to dash,
                O how unfit!

But mak the Rustic, haggis-fed,
The trembling earth resounds his tread,
Clap in his wallie nieve a blade,
                He'll mak it whissle;
An' legs, an' arms, an heads will sned,
                Like taps o' thrissle.

Ye Pow'rs wha mak mankind your care,
And dish them out their bill o' fare,
Auld Scotland wants nae skinking ware
                That jaups in luggies;
But, if ye wish her gratefu' prayer
                Gie her a Haggis!

IDAHO[37]
By John McMillan

Idaho a land out in the West
It's the place that I love best
Tis the Country where all settling ought to go
For the crops you can not beat
And the mountains skies do meet.
And for climates it is Idaho
Where the living waters flow
And the choicest taters grow
Anywhere that you may go in Idaho
We got tired of part where the gomets sure do frast.

And we're looking for a good place to go
We have travelled thru the West where
The wordy are the best
So we'r living out here in Idaho.
        ########
When next time we do meet new faces you will greet.
As a meeting such as this does clearly show.
So we'll pat you on the back and we hope you'll understand
For we need you out in Idaho.

Beautiful, Beautiful Boise
By John McMillan

At the eastern end of a stub line you know,
Lies the Capitol city of (all) Idaho,
        It's beautiful beautiful Boise.

Clinging close to the mountains hills covered with snow,
In a peaceful vale where the winds rarely blow,
        Lies Beautiful, beautiful Boise.

There's a snug little city for strangers to scan,
Lying twenty miles west from Arrow rock Dam,
        That's beautiful, beautiful Boise.

There the choicest fruit in the whole valley grows,
And the boiling hot springs from lava rock flows,
        At beautiful, beautiful Boise.

For forty odd years from the world we've been hid
But now we're determined to raise up the lid
        At beautiful beautiful Boise.
Now forty long years is an awful long time,
for people to ry to get on the "Main Line",
        At beautiful, beautiful Boise.

But now we're assured that it's certainly so
And tourists in future will know how to go
          To beautiful beautiful Boise.
As the short line train through the sagebrush reels,
The traveler "looks out" for the "depot's on wheels,"
          At beautiful, beautiful Boise.

But now as the traveler a long breath does draw,
He peacefully sleeps at the Idanha-ha,
          In beautiful beautiful Boise
His traveling companion, not so wise as he,
Still wandering around at the Owyhee-hee
          In beautiful beautiful Boise.

The following column regarding John McMillans' writing of verse appeared
in the *Idaho Statesman* newspaper, date unknown:

"Writer of Rhymes With Poor Opinion of farming in Idaho"

"Unburdens his soul on Scrap of Paper in Lobby of a Boise Hotel and
Escapes."

"John McMillan tells a bit of a story that is woven about a scrap of verse
scribbled apparently at random on an old envelope of hotel stationery that
runs as follows:

"I sat down at a writing desk at the Idanha not long ago to write a letter
or two. I sat at the desk trying to decide just what I wished to say in my
first letter, turning the matter over in my mind, when a bit of scribbling
on an old envelope attracted my attention. The envelope was of the hotel
stationery and the writing was in sort of careless scrawl. Both sides of the
envelope were written full and I guess it was it was this quantity production
on an envelope that caused me to look closer and then to try and decipher
the writing. Finally I made out the following:

"Farm work is hard work sure . . .
Tired bones and muscles are hard to endure . . .
At night you seek your weary couch . . .

At five in the morn' you awake with a grouch.
You work all day until nin or half past.
And wonder at such a rate how long you'll last.
It may do for youth but for one past sixty-three
It is wearing and may soon set a busy soul free.
I find ranch work continuous drudgery
And the pay of a country gentleman humbuggery . . .
Perhaps I do not get it right
But indeed the work piles up clear out of sight.
Surely I'll give this work a fair test
Hoping that I may find some time to rest;
Just now every job is a different task . . .
Plowing, planting, howing and hay to mow.
So the work moves on in a continuous Flow."

At the time I was working my ranch at Murphy and had just driven in
from the place. I was a bit of the same mind as the writer of the poetry, but
on thinking the proposition over further, I decided he might be just a sort
of chronic kicker to whom any work would be distasteful so I added the
following two lines to his envelope full of verse and left it:

"Till the end of time we are made to work, so what are you kicking at you
lazy Turk?"

Is McMillan Guilty?

"The verses in the *Statesman* Saturday have been causing much comment
in the literary circles of the city [Boise.] The poetic lines were reported to
have been found on an old envelope in the Idanha Hotel, written by some
unknown author in a dejected moment.

Several of Mr. McMillan's friends however, claim that he himself spent
several days in the quiet of his offices penning those lines. In days gone by
Mr. McMillan was considered an orator of no mean ability, and his friends
are hoping that his recent effort will encourage him to pursue the role of
poet further."[38]

CHAPTER TEN

JOHN MCMILLAN'S DEATH

"John McMillan Idaho pioneer dies in Oregon."

"Word was received Wednesday of the death of John McMillan, 79, formerly a prominent Boise businessman and livestock grower, who died in Portland,[Oregon] where he has been living since he left Idaho a year and a half ago. Mr. McMillan, who lived in Boise nearly 50 years, was a former member of both branches of the Idaho Legislature, a Boise postmaster and a leader in Republican circles. Death came after a lingering illness. Although he was not associated with the institution at the time of his death, Mr. McMillan was one of the stockholders that build and controlled the Idanha Hotel."[39]

ENDNOTES

1. Certificate of Entry of Birth, Parish of Minigraff in the Stewartry of Kirkudbright, date of extract, May 25, 1857.

2. From the Foreword of the booklet titled *"A Stroll Around Kirkudbright"*, published by the Kirkcudbright Rotary Club in June 1973, the work of the History Department of Kirkcudbright Academy,

3. From *http://www.old-kirkudbright.net/*, An Internet Browse Through the History topography and Genealogy of the Ancient Parish and Burgh of Kirkcudbright, taken from a selection of contemporary books, magazines, documents, maps, illustrations and ephemera., 10/7/2007.

4. H.T. French, *History of Idaho*, 1914, p. 601-602.

5. Sheep Wars: Information from Answers.com. *U.S. History Encyclopedia.*

6. From the City of Mountain Home web site [*http://www.mountain-home.us/*]

7. The Idanha Hotel has in recent years been rehabbed for retail and apartment use: Information from *Planning*, the magazine of the American Planning Association, July 2003.

8. News Release: October 4, 2004, The Office of communications and Marketing, Boise State University, regarding a photo exhibit titled "Idanha's Trial of the Century" which was to be shown in the Lobby of the Idanha Hotel in downtown Boise, Idaho.

5. *daho Daily Statesman*, November 22, 1886.

6. Births Deaths, Marriages, "Funeral" *Idaho Daily Statesman*, date unknown.

7. "John McMillan, Idaho Pioneer Dies in Oregon," *Idaho Daily Statesman*, July 9, 1936, pp. 1,6.

8. Certificate of Entry of Birth, Parish of Minnigraff in the Stewartry of Kirkudbright, date of extract, May 25, 1857.

9. "Clara H. McMillan Dies Unexpectedly At Home In Boise," *Idaho Daily Statesman*, date unknown.

10. H.T. French, *History of Idaho*, 1914, p. 602.

11. From a column in the *Idaho Daily Statesman*, unknown date in 1918.

12. Jane Stewart, late of 1222 N. E. Schuyler Street, Portland, Oregon, died at age 83, mother of Agnes I. Brown, Salmon, Idaho, Charles Stewart, Idaho Falls, Idaho, and Mary Stewart, Portland, sister of Thomas McMillan and Mary Aikman, Boise, Idaho, and John McMillan, Portland. Friends were invited to attend funeral services at Holman & Lutz Colonial Mortuary, 14th and Sandy Blvd., Portland on November 30 at 10:00 a.m., with interment at Rose City Cemetary., from a column in the Portland Oregonian, date unknown.

13. *Idaho Daily Statesman*, June 22, 1935

14. "Robert Aikman Pioneer Idaho Sheepman, Dies," *Idaho Daily Statesman*, date unknown.

15. "Scab and Scabby," a column in the *Idaho Daily Statesman*, date unknown

16. "Cattle associations, organizations of cattlemen after 1865 on the western ranges, local, district, sectional, and national in scope functioned on the edges of western Angle-American settlements, much lik miner's associations and squatters' claim clubs. The Colorado Cattle Growers' Association was formed as early as 1867. The Wyoming Stock Growers' association was organized in 1873 and by 1886 had four hundred members from nineteen states. Its cattle, real estate, plants and horses were valued in 1885 at $100 million. In 1884 the National cattle and Horse Growers' assoication was organized in St. Louis," *US History Encyclopedia*, from Answers.com. date unknown.

17. From several columns in the *Idaho Daily Statesman*, dates unknown.

18. From a column in the *Idaho Daily Statesman*, date unknown.

19. From a column in the *Idaho Daily Statesman*, accompanied by a photo of McMillan, date unknown.

20. "Short Biographical Items Regarding Hon. W.E. Borah," A column in the *Idaho Daily statesman*, January 14, 1907

21. "William E. Borah", *Britannica Online Encylcopedia*.

22. Ibid.

23. From a column in the *Idaho Daily Statesman*, January 16, 1907

24. Ibid.

25. Ibid.

26. From a column in the *Idaho Daily Statesman*, date unknown.

27. From a column in the *Idaho statesman* (a notice!)

28. Richenda Miers, *Scotish Life Magazine*, Autumn 2007, p. 34.

29. Ibid.

"Reference to the John Knox Tree is probably referring to The Great Yew of Ormiston, a first class example of the few layering yews known in Scotland. Weeping branches radiate out from the central trunk and take root where they touch the ground. This tree could be as old as 1000 years. It is considered a 15th century landmark. "As early as the 15th century the yew was recognized as a local landmark. A parchment dated 1474 found among some old papers belonging to the Earl of Hopetoun, had been signed under the yew tree.

"The famous religious reformer, John Knox who was born in nearby Haddington, is also reputed to have preached his early sermons within the secluded interior of the yew's evergreen canopy. Here Knox, along with his influential mentor, George Wishart, sowed the seeds of the Reformation, which was ultimately to sweep throughout Scotland." Http//www.forestry. gov.uk/forestry/INFD-6UEHNQ, 2/3/2009, p. 1

30. Ibid, p. 39.

31. *Act of Naturalization* [Citizenship] papers, March 15, 1890. p. 1.

32. It would appear that the author and her father should have been spelling their name MacMillan rather than McMillan, in accordance with his fathers' and her grandfathers' naturalization/citizenship papers of 1890 !!

33. D. MacDonell MacDonald, "These are your people. The MacMillans, Children of the Tonsured servant", a Reprint from *The Highlander*, p 1-2.

34. Ibid.

35. From a column in *Scotish Life Magazine*, date unknown.

36. Words by John McMillan, Boise, Idaho, and music by L.S. Edwards, Baker City, Oregon. Dated November 12, 1904.

37. This poem was handwritten on the back of a Monthly Report form for McMILLAN'S RANCH, Date unknown.

38. From a column in the *Idaho Daily Statesman*, date unknown.

39. From the Idaho Daily Statesman, Thursday, July 9, 1936, pp. 1 & 6.

www.ingramcontent.com/pod-product-compliance
Lightning Source LLC
Chambersburg PA
CBHW061223280526
45784CB00006B/2612